PALEO SEAFOOD COOKER

30 SIMPLE GRAIN-FREE SLOW COOKER RECIPES FOR BEGINNERS

TABLE OF CONTENTS

Introduction

I want to thank you and congratulate you for downloading the book, *"Paleo Seafood Slow Cooker: 30 Simple Grain-Free Slow Cooker Recipes for Beginners"*.

This book contains proven steps and strategies on how to prepare and serve delicious seafood dinners that taste like they were made by a pro, with little to no effort.

With this book, you will learn how to create delicious dinners you and your whole family will enjoy.   You'll look forward to seafood night when you head into it armed with the thirty tasty recipes outlined in this book!

Thanks again for downloading this book, I hope you enjoy it!

Chapter 1 - How Seafood Helps

Seafood and Weight Loss

Seafood is one of the healthiest food groups you can consume. It is full of omega-3 fatty acids, which are vital nutrients that your body needs in order to continue functioning appropriately. Omega-3s can help reduce the risk of heart attack, stroke, and death related to other forms of heart failure; they can also significantly increase your ability to lose weight quickly and keep it off. They are also great for helping reduce the buildup of plaque in the arteries, which again contributes to the overall health of your heart and your physical ability to exercise more, thus leading to even more weight loss benefits.

Omega-3s are also great for reducing inflammation in your body. When you reduce painful inflammation, such as from arthritis or even inflamed bowel problems, you are sure to feel better, be less bloated, exercise more, and lose weight much more easily. And seafood is the leading food group that contains these vital fatty acids!

Seafood also is incredibly low in carbohydrates (containing slim to none), low in fats, low in cholesterol, and low in caloric content. You are truly doing your body a huge favor when you consume fish, shellfish, and other forms of seafood!

It is important to eat fish or other seafood as often as possible. Even a small serving of fish is great for you, and it keeps you feeling focused, healthy, and ready to take on the world!

Seafood and Paleo Style

Seafood fits very smoothly into a paleo lifestyle and its accompanying diet. The paleo diet focuses on the types and variety of foods that would have been consumed by early hunter-gatherers. This means that paleo dieters consume anything that could have been grown, hunted, foraged, or otherwise easily located by hunter-gatherer societies. This is where the term "paleo" comes from—it refers to the word "paleolithic." This diet focuses largely on meats, vegetables, fruits, nuts, and spices. It relies on honey and natural brown sugar as sweeteners, and advises avoiding sugar, grains, corn, and refined or highly processed forms of any food. Dairy and eggs are permissible by the paleo diet, but if you choose to avoid dairy and/or eggs, this is an easy diet to modify to that type of lifestyle, too.

The act of catching fish to cook and eat dates back over forty thousand years. Fish hooks have even been found dating back to the stone age—in more or less the same shape as fish hooks that we use today! Fishing is one of the earliest forms of obtaining meat and proteins in the diet, which means that fish and seafood are excellent candidates for paleo dieting. If early man (and woman) would have eaten fish and seafood, then we should be eating them, too!

However, the key to keeping to a paleo diet is all in the preparation of these foods. They should be kept away from grains and processed foods, and should always be served with vegetables to keep your meal balanced and your paleo diet going strong. In this way, you are sure to lose weight quickly, keep it off, and live a healthy lifestyle all the way around!

An important point to remember about cooking seafood in the slow cooker is that, unlike many other slow cooker recipes, it should not be left alone all day to cook! Seafood slow cooker recipes generally only take a few hours until they are complete, so be sure you will be home to turn off the heat when necessary.

Garlic Tilapia

This is a simple recipe that kids and adults are both sure to enjoy. The delightful flavor of the garlic works beautifully with the simple butter coating to ensure that this fish is flavorful and juicy every time.

4 filets of tilapia

2 tbsp butter at room temperature

2 tbsp minced garlic

Black pepper to taste

1. Stir minced garlic into butter until well combined.

2. Tear off four square of tin foil large enough to wrap up each filet of tilapia.

3. Place a filet into each square and season with black pepper.

4. Rub each fish with garlic butter and wrap tightly in tin foil.

5. Place or stack foil-covered filets into slow cooker.

6. Cover and cook on high for 2 hours.

7. Serve.

Asian Salmon

If you're looking for a healthy way to enjoy the flavors of Asian cuisine, look no further than this tasty salmon with Asian style seasonings.   Serve up with a bag of steamed frozen Asian vegetable medley for a perfect meal!

10oz filet of salmon

16oz frozen Asian stir fry vegetables

Black pepper to taste

2 tbsp soy sauce (or coconut aminos, if you prefer to avoid soy)

2 tbsp honey

2 tbsp lemon juice

1 tsp sesame seeds (optional)

1. Place frozen vegetables into slow cooker.

2. Season salmon filet(s) with black pepper to taste, then place fish on top of frozen vegetables in slow cooker.

3. In a small bowl, stir together soy sauce, honey, and lemon juice; drizzle mixture over fish.

4. Sprinkle sesame seeds over fish.

5. Cover and cook on low for 2 hours.

6. Serve.

Salmon Bake

With only a few ingredients, this recipe proves to be one of the simplest and yet most flavorful dishes available for salmon slow cooking. It stands alone perfectly well, and goes great with cauliflower rice, too!

2 chicken bouillon cubes

1 cup boiling water

16oz canned salmon

2 cups seasoned croutons for stuffing

1 cup shredded cheddar cheese

2 eggs

1/4 tsp dry mustard

1. In a small bowl, beat eggs.

2. Dissolve bouillon cubes into boiling water.

3. Drain and flake canned salmon.

4. Place croutons into the bottom of the slow cooker.

5. Pour over chicken stock and beaten eggs; stir well.

6. Add canned salmon, cheddar cheese, and dry mustard.

7. Stir well to combine all ingredients.

8. Cover and cook on high for 2 hours.

9. Serve.

Cheesy Tilapia

Everyone loves a little cheese in their meals! Enjoy the added bonus of dairy when you make this tasty tilapia.

4 filets of tilapia

1/4 cup mayonnaise

1/2 cup shredded cheddar cheese

2 lemons

3 tbsp minced garlic

Black pepper to taste

1. Juice lemons.

2. Tear off four squares of tin foil and place a fish filet into the center of each one.

3. In a small bowl, combine mayonnaise, cheddar cheese, lemon juice, garlic, and black pepper; stir well.

4. Spread mixture over each of the four fish filets.

5. Close tin foil packets around fish filets and place or stack in slow cooker.

6. Cover and cook on low for 3 hours.

Mexican Style Salmon

If you're looking for a slightly spicy fish recipe, this is the salmon for you! You are sure to enjoy the way the cilantro combines with the other spices in this recipe to create a Latin taste.

4 salmon filets

3/4 cup fresh cilantro

2 tbsp minced garlic

1 lime

1 tbsp olive oil

1. Remove stems from cilantro and chop leaves finely.

2. Juice lime.

3. Rub slow cooker crock with half of the olive oil.

4. Place filets into slow cooker; try not to stack, if possible.

5. In a small bowl, stir together cilantro, garlic, lime juice, and remaining olive oil.

6. Pour mixture over fish in slow cooker.

7. Cover and cook on high for 1 hour.

8. Serve.

Citrusy Halibut

This fresh summertime fish recipe is great for those dinners when you want something cool and refreshing to eat. After cooking in the slow cooker, optionally let it cool and then flake it into a citrus salad!

2 pounds filet of halibut

Black pepper to taste

1 onion

1/4 cup fresh parsley

4 tsp olive oil

1 lemon

1 orange

1. Chop onion and parsley.

2. Grate rind from lemon and orange; save fruit to serve in a citrus salad or alongside the cooked fish.

3. Season fish with black pepper and place into slow cooker.

4. Sprinkle fish with parsley, onion, olive oil, and citrus rinds.

5. Cover and cook for 2 hours on low.

6. Serve.

Maple Glazed Salmon

This salmon recipe is a hearty fall meal that will keep you warm on a chilly day. The maple syrup will remind you of New England and the delicious flavors of autumn.

6 filets of salmon

1/2 cup pure maple syrup

1 lime

1/4 cup soy sauce (or coconut aminos)

1 tbsp minced garlic

1 tsp dried ginger

1. Juice lime.

2. Place salmon into slow cooker.

3. In a small bowl, combine maple syrup, lime juice, soy sauce, garlic, and ginger.

4. Pour sauce over fish.

5. Cover and cook on low for 1 hour.

6. Serve.

Dill Dijon Salmon

Dill weed is an excellent way to season your meals without adding any unwanted side effects or ingredients, but still enjoying maximum flavor payout!

1 onion

1 tbsp minced garlic

4 tbsp olive oil

2 cups water

2 cubes chicken bouillon

1 tsp dried dill weed

1-1/2 pounds filet of salmon

Black pepper to taste

1/3 cup Dijon mustard

1 lemon

1/3 cup plain yogurt

1. Dice onion finely.

2. In a microwave safe bowl, stir together onion, 1/2 tbsp minced garlic, and 1 tbsp olive oil; microwave on high for 4 minutes, then stir again and pour into slow cooker.

3. Pour water, bouillon cubes, and dill weed into slow cooker and stir to dissolve bouillon.

4. Season the salmon filets with pepper to taste.

5. Place fish on top of mixture in slow cooker.

6. Cover and cook on low for 2 hours.

7. Juice lemon.

8. In a small bowl, combine Dijon mustard, lemon juice, plain yogurt, 3 tbsp olive oil, and 1/2 tbsp minced garlic, and whisk together to combine thoroughly.

9. Serve salmon filets topped with Dijon sauce.

Salmon Loaf

Love meatloaf but hate how fattening ground beef can be? Use salmon instead and cook up a yummy salmon loaf that will be great as leftovers on a sandwich, too!

15oz canned salmon

2 eggs

2 cups herbed croutons for stuffing

1 cup shredded (or grated) Parmesan cheese

1 cup chicken broth

1/4 cup French onions

1 tsp dry mustard

Black pepper to taste

1. Drain canned salmon and remove any skin or bones.

2. Beat eggs into a small bowl.

3. Crush French onions.

4. In a large bowl, stir together croutons, eggs, cheese, chicken broth, French onions, mustard, and black pepper.

5. Add canned salmon and stir together again.

6. Pat into a round loaf.

7. Place loaf into slow cooker.

8. Cover and cook on low for 4 hours.

9. Serve.

Au Gratin White Fish

Any white fish will do for this recipe, but tilapia works especially well!   This is a recipe that appears to be fancy but really isn't difficult to make at all!

3 pounds white fish filets

6 tbsp butter

3 tbsp almond flour

1/2 tbsp dry mustard

1/4 tbsp nutmeg

1-1/4 cup milk

1 lemon

1 cup shredded cheddar cheese

1. Juice lemon.

2. Melt butter in a microwave-safe bowl until just melted.

3. Stir almond flour, mustard, and nutmeg into butter.

4. Slowly add milk while stirring constantly to thicken mixture.

5. Stir in lemon juice and cheese until cheese is melted.

6. Place fish into slow cooker and pour sauce over fish.

7. Cover and cook on high for 1 hour.

8. Serve.

Shrimp Casserole

Use cauliflower to make "rice" that you can serve up easily with this delicious shrimp casserole! This is a surprisingly hearty meal that will leave you feeling full and happy afterward.

1-1/2 pounds frozen pre-cooked shrimp

1 head cauliflower

1 cup chicken broth

1 can cream of celery soup

1 can cream of chicken soup

1 can diced tomatoes

1 onion

1 red bell pepper

1 yellow bell pepper

Black pepper to taste

Dried parsley to taste

1 tbsp garlic powder

1. Devein shrimp, peel, and pull off tails.

2. Chop onion and both bell peppers.

3. Place cauliflower into a blender; blend on high until cauliflower reaches a rice-like consistency.

4. Place cauliflower rice into slow cooker.

5. Arrange shrimp on top of rice.

6. Pour over chicken broth, both soups, diced tomatoes, vegetables, and spices.

7. Stir to mix everything together thoroughly.

8. Cover and cook on low for 6 hours.

9. Serve.

Sweet and Sour Shrimp

This recipe creates a simple Asian style dish that is very traditional and very loved by many people!   Serve with Asian veggies or salad with ginger dressing.

6oz frozen edamame

13oz canned pineapple chunks in juice

2 tbsp corn starch

3 tbsp brown sugar

1 chicken bouillon cube

1 cup boiling water

1/2 cup juice from canned pineapple

2 tsp soy sauce (or coconut aminos)

1/2 tsp dried ginger

9oz canned shrimp

2 tbsp apple cider vinegar

1. Place edamame and drained pineapple into slow cooker.

2. Stir corn starch and brown sugar together in a small skillet on the stove over medium-high heat.

3. Add bouillon cube, boiling water, pineapple juice, soy sauce, and ginger; stir to combine thoroughly and dissolve bouillon cube.

4. Cook for 1 minute or until thick.

5. Stir sauce into slow cooker.

6. Cover and cook on low for 4 hours.

7. Drain canned shrimp and stir into mixture.

8. Serve.

Lemon Shrimp

Here is another great use for cauliflower "rice"! This is a very simple dish with just a few key ingredients that make it taste amazing.

2 lemons

30oz chicken broth

1/2 cup white wine (optional)

2 tsp butter

2 tsp olive oil

1 shallot

1 head cauliflower

1 cup frozen peas

1 pound frozen shrimp

Black pepper to taste

1. Juice lemons and grate rind.

2. Mince shallot finely.

3. Place cauliflower into a blender; blend on high until cauliflower reaches a rice-like consistency.

4. Peel, devein, and remove tail from frozen shrimp.

5. In a large pot on the stove over high heat, place lemon juice, wine, and water to a boil.

6. In a large microwave safe bowl, place butter, olive oil, and shallot; microwave for 2 minutes on high and stir to mix well.

7. Add cauliflower rice to butter mixture and stir to coat.

8. Stir hot liquid mixture into butter mixture.

9. Pour entire mixture into slow cooker and stir in frozen peas, shrimp, and black pepper.

10. Cover and cook on low for 1 hour.

11. Serve.

Lime Chili Shrimp

This tasty Latin-inspired shrimp tastes great over a salad of dark, leafy greens! Help yourself to plenty of these yummy shrimp.

1 pound frozen shrimp

1/4 cup olive oil

1 lime

1 tsp chili powder

2 tbsp minced garlic

Black pepper to taste

1. Peel, devein, and remove tail from shrimp.

2. Juice lime.

3. Place shrimp into the slow cooker.

4. Pour over lime juice, olive oil, chili powder, garlic, and black pepper; stir to combine flavors well and coat shrimp.

5. Cover and cook on low for 2 hours.

6. Serve.

Crawfish Combo

Crawfish isn't a shrimp itself, but it is closely related. Combined in this recipe with shrimp, it makes for a great flavor that tastes amazing over salad, cauliflower rice, zucchini noodles, or simply with a side of asparagus!

1 pound uncooked fresh shrimp

1 onion

1 red bell pepper

4 green onions

2 stalks celery

1/4 cup butter

2 tbsp minced garlic

1 tbsp almond flour

15oz canned diced tomatoes

10oz canned tomatoes and green chiles

6oz canned tomato paste

2/3 cup water

1 pound pre-cooked, peeled crawfish tails

1 tsp dried basil

1 tsp dried thyme

1 tsp dried oregano

1 tsp black pepper

1/4 tsp red pepper flakes

1 tbsp dried parsley

1. Peel and devein shrimp.
2. Dice onion and red bell pepper.
3. Slice green onions and celery stalks.

4. In a large skillet on the stove over medium-high heat, melt better.

5. Add onion, red bell pepper, green onion, celery, and garlic; cook for 5 minutes.

6. Add almond flour and cook for 1 minute, stirring constantly until smooth.

7. Add diced tomatoes, tomatoes and green chiles, tomato paste, and water; stir well.

8. Add basil, thyme, oregano, black pepper, parsley, and red pepper flakes; stir well.

9. Pour mixture into slow cooker.

10. Cover and cook on low for 4 hours.

11. Add crawfish and shrimp; cover and cook on low for 1 additional hour.

12. Serve.

Shrimp Marinara

Mix up a batch of this shrimp marinara to serve over your next spaghetti squash noodles!

1 can peeled tomatoes

2 tbsp dried parsley

1 tbsp minced garlic

1 tsp dried basil

Black pepper to taste

1 tsp dried oregano

6oz canned tomato paste

1 pound pre-cooked frozen shrimp

1. Shell, devein, and remove tails from shrimp.

2. Dice peeled tomatoes.

3. Place tomatoes into slow cooker with parsley, garlic, basil, black pepper, oregano, and tomato paste; stir to combine well.

4. Cover and cook on low for 6 hours.

5. Add shrimp and stir.

6. Cover and cook on low for 15 minutes.

7. Serve.

Barbecue Shrimp

This yummy Cajun style shrimp takes almost no time to prepare and works great in a multitude of different meals!

2 tbsp minced garlic

1 tsp Cajun seasoning

1/2 cup butter

1/4 cup Worcestershire sauce

1 tbsp tabasco sauce

1 lemon

Black pepper to taste

1-1/2 pounds large shrimp

1 green onion

1. Cut butter into pieces.

2. Finely chop green onion.

3. Juice lemon.

4. Stir together garlic, Cajun seasoning, butter, Worcestershire sauce, tabasco sauce, and lemon juice in the slow cooker.

5. Add black pepper.

6. Cover and cook for 30 minutes on high.

7. Rinse and drain shrimp in the meantime.

8. Remove and save 1/2 of the sauce from the slow cooker.

9. Place shrimp into the remaining sauce and drizzle with reserved half.

10. Stir to coat shrimp thoroughly.

11. Cover and cook on high for 30 minutes.

12. Sprinkle with green onion and serve.

Shrimp Fondue

This one also includes scallops, but relies heavily on the shrimp to provide the delicious taste.   Use it for dipping fresh veggies and you will have a very exciting, high-class meal no one will believe you didn't spend all day preparing!

22oz condensed cream of celery soup

2 cups shredded cheddar cheese

1-1/2 cup chopped cooked shrimp

1/2 cup shopped cooked scallops

Dash of paprika

Dash of cayenne pepper

1. Pour soup into slow cooker.

2. Add cheese, paprika, and cayenne pepper; stir to combine thoroughly.

3. Stir in shrimp and scallops.

4. Cover and cook on high for 1 hour.

5. Serve.

Bacon Shrimp Chowder

Enjoy this hearty soup on a cold winter's day and warm up yourself and your whole family!   Just be sure to make plenty for seconds or leftovers—this one is a popular dish!

1 pound pre-cooked frozen shrimp

4oz bacon

1 onion

1 pound potatoes

1 pint milk

1/2 pint water

1 tbsp Worcestershire sauce

1 tbsp almond flour

1. Peel, devein, and remove tails from shrimp.

2. Peel and dice onion and potatoes.

3. Fry bacon to desired doneness in a large skillet on the stove over medium-high heat.

4. Remove bacon from skillet and dice.

5. Add potato to bacon grease and cook for 5 minutes.

6. Add onions and cook for 5 minutes more.

7. Place mixture into slow cooker.

8. Chop shrimp into smaller chunks and place into slow cooker.

9. Cover and cook on low for 5 hours.

10. Combine flour and milk and stir into slow cooker to thicken chowder.

11. Cook uncovered on low for 30 minutes more.

12. Serve.

Garlic Shrimp

This tasty recipe works best in a slow cooker, since the low temperature and extended cooking time can keep the shrimp from becoming overcooked and tough.

3/4 cup olive oil

3 tbsp minced garlic

1 tsp paprika

Black pepper to taste

1/4 tsp red pepper flakes

2 pounds raw shrimp

1. Peel, devein, and remove tails from shrimp.

2. Stir together olive oil, garlic, paprika, black pepper, and red pepper flakes into the slow cooker.

3. Cover and cook on high for 30 minutes.

4. Stir shrimp into mixture and coat thoroughly.

5. Cover and cook on high for 10 minutes; stir again.

6. Cover and cook on high for another 10 minutes.

7. Serve.

Crab Legs

If you love steamed crab legs, you'll adore how easy they are to make in the slow cooker! Pair them with cauliflower rice, spaghetti squash noodles, or fresh steamed veggies!

3 bunches of snow crab legs

1/2 cup butter

4 tbsp minced garlic

1 tsp dill

1. Rinse crab legs under cool water.

2. Place crab legs into slow cooker and cover halfway with water.

3. Melt butter in a small, microwave safe bowl and stir in garlic and dill.

4. Pour mixture over crab legs.

5. Cover and cook on low for 2 hours.

6. Serve.

Crab and Artichoke Dip

This yummy, crab dip is great for parties—and it tastes a lot fancier than it really is. You can make it in no time with just a few, simple ingredients!

14oz canned artichoke hearts

8oz cream cheese

4oz canned crab meat

1/2 cup grated Parmesan

4 green onions

1 lemon

1. Juice lemon.

2. Thinly slice green onions.

3. Drain and flake crab meat.

4. Drain and chop artichoke hearts.

5. Place artichoke hearts into slow cooker.

6. Stir in cream cheese, carb meat, Parmesan, green onions, and lemon juice.

7. Cover and cook on low for 2 hours.

8. Stir until smooth.

9. Serve.

Easy Crab Dip

For any holiday, family get-together, or party, whip up a batch of this warm crab dip and wow everybody!

1 pound soft block cheese

1 pound butter

2 cans crab meat

1. Drain crab meat and flake; remove cartilage or shell pieces.

2. Place block cheese, butter, and crab meat into slow cooker.

3. Cover and cook on low for 4 hours or until cheese melts thoroughly; be sure to stir periodically while cooking.

4. Serve.

Crabs in Cooking Sherry

This recipe puts a unique take on crab meat with the spicy and oh so savory addition of cooking sherry and Worcestershire sauce.

26oz canned crab meat

20oz canned cream of mushroom soup

6 tbsp butter

1/4 cup dry cooking sherry

1/2 tsp Worcestershire sauce

1/2 cup light sour cream

Black pepper to taste

3 green onions

2 eggs

1. In a small bowl, beat eggs lightly.

2. Finely chop green onion.

3. Drain and flake crab meat.

4. Place crab into slow cooker and pour over mushroom soup, butter, cooking sherry, Worcestershire sauce, sour cream, black pepper, and green onions.

5. Cover and cook on low for 3 hours.

6. Stir in eggs; cover and cook on low for 1 hour   more.

7. Serve.

Crab Casserole

Nothing beats a hot, heaping helping of delicious crab casserole on a cold day!

3 tbsp butter

2 stalks celery

1 onion

1 green bell pepper

3 tbsp almond flour

3 chicken bouillon cubes

2-1/2 cups boiling water

1 head cauliflower

14oz canned crab meat

2-1/2 cups shredded Swiss cheese

14oz canned sliced mushrooms

1/4 cup sliced pimientos and green olives

1. Chop celery, onion, and green bell pepper.

2. Drain and flake crab meat.

3. Drain mushrooms.

4. In a large skillet over medium-high heat, melt butter and cook celery, onion, and green bell pepper for 5 minutes.

5. Stir in almond flour.

6. Dissolve bouillon cubes into boiling water and pour into a skillet.

7. Bring everything in the skillet to a boil while stirring continuously; cook for 2 minutes more.

8. Place cauliflower into a blender; blend on high until cauliflower is a rice like consistency.

9. Combine cauliflower rice with crab meat, 2 cups Swiss cheese, sliced mushrooms, and pimientos and green olives in the slow cooker.

10. Pour sauce over everything in slow cooker and stir to combine thoroughly.

11. Cover and cook on high for 3 hours.

12. Top with remaining shredded cheese and serve.

Lobster Bisque

Anyone who loves lobster is sure to enjoy a delicious, warming, hearty lobster bisque. This recipe makes for a great one!

2 shallots

1 tbsp minced garlic

30oz canned diced tomatoes

32oz chicken broth

1 tbsp oregano

1 tsp dill weed

1/4 cup fresh parsley

1 tsp black pepper

1/2 tsp paprika

4 lobster tails

1 pint heavy cream

1. Mince shallots finely.

2. Chop parsley.

3. Place shallots and garlic into a microwave safe bowl; microwave on high for 3 minutes.

4. Place mixture into the slow cooker and pour in tomatoes (with juice), chicken broth, oregano, dill weed, parsley, pepper, and paprika.

5. Stir to combine flavors.

6. Cover and cook on high for 3 hours.

7. Pour mixture into blender and puree to desired smoothness.

8. Pour back into slow cooker.

9. Add lobster tails, cover, and cook on low for 45 minutes.

10. Remove tails.

11. Add cream and stir into soup.

12. Cut shells in half and remove flesh from tails.

13. Chop lobster meat and stir into soup.

14. Serve.

Lobster Chowder

Enjoy the yummy New England flavor of lobster bisque any time of the year—especially in the winter!

1-1/2 pound cooked lobster meat

3-1/2 cup potatoes

1 onion

1 tsp paprika

1 tsp cumin

1 tsp thyme

1 tsp basil

1 tsp black pepper

1 tsp minced garlic

1 jalapeño pepper

4 slices bacon

1-1/2 cup lobster stock

3-1/2 cup half and half

1. Peel and cube potatoes.

2. Dice jalapeño pepper.

3. Cook bacon in a large skillet over medium-high heat to desired doneness, then set aside bacon and reserve grease.

4. Stir potatoes, onion, spices, jalapeño pepper, lobster stock, and half and half into slow cooker.

5. Pour bacon grease into slow cooker.

6. Cover and cook on high for 4 hours.

7. Dice lobster meat and place into slow cooker; stir gently.

8. Cover and cook on high for 1 hour more.

9. Serve sprinkled with chopped bacon.

Lobster Tails

Like crab legs, lobster tails don't have to be complicated or difficult to make. All you need is your slow cooker and some liquid, and you'll be ready to go!

4 lobster tails

8oz water

4oz dry white wine

1/2 stick butter

4 tbsp minced garlic

1. Place lobster tails into slow cooker.
2. Pour water over lobster tails.
3. In a small bowl, melt butter and stir in garlic.
4. Pour over lobster tails in slow cooker.
5. Add white wine.
6. Cover and cook on high for 1 hour.
7. Serve.

Cauliflower Lobster

In place of risotto or rice, use cauliflower rice to jazz up your lobster dish.

1 head cauliflower

4 tbsp olive oil

1 onion

3/4 cup dry white wine

4-1/4 cup vegetable broth

16oz lobster tails

1 cup cherry tomatoes

1/4 cup spinach

Black pepper to taste

Cayenne pepper to taste

1. Place cauliflower into blender; blend on high until cauliflower reaches a rice-like consistency.

2. Slice fresh spinach.

3. Remove and dice meat from lobster tails.

4. Halve cherry tomatoes.

5. Dice onion.

6. In a large skillet over medium heat, cook onion and cauliflower rice in olive oil for 5 minutes.

7. Add white wine and simmer until reduced halfway.

8. Pour mixture into slow cooker and pour over vegetable broth, stirring once.

9. Cover and cook on high for 1 hour.

10. Add lobster and stir to combine.

11. Cover and cook on high for 10 minutes.

12. Stir in tomatoes, spinach, black pepper, and cayenne pepper.

13. Serve.

Lobster Scampi

Serve this lobster dish with a side of spaghetti squash noodles for a delightful, light dinner!

10oz cooked lobster meat

1/2 stick butter

1/2 cup olive oil

4 tbsp minced garlic

1 tsp paprika

2 tbsp Worcestershire sauce

1/2 cup dry white wine

1 lemon

1. Juice lemon.

2. In a large skillet over medium high heat, melt butter and olive oil and cook garlic.

3. Stir in Worcestershire, white wine, and paprika, and cook for 5 minutes.

4. Stir in lemon juice and pour liquids into slow cooker.

5. Stir lobster meat into liquids in slow cooker.

6. Cover and cook on low for 1 hour.

7. Serve.

Conclusion

Thank you again for downloading this book!

I hope this book was able to help you to learn all about how to prepare seafood in the slow cooker.

The next step is to pick your favorite recipe and start cooking!

Made in the USA
Middletown, DE
06 December 2017